The Swearing Parrot

— *and Other Rhymes* —

Rhymes by Joan Hoogewerf

Illustrations by Thalia Apostolopoulos

The Swearing Parrot and Other Rhymes

Illustrations:
Thalia Apostolopoulos

Wholesale discounts for book orders are available through Ingram Distributors.

Tellwell Talent
www.tellwell.ca

ISBN
Paperback: 978-1-77370-205-6
Hardcover: 978-1-77370-206-3

The Swearing Parrot and Other Rhymes

On 'Wobbly Wednesdays' these rhymes were written by a grandmother and illustrated by her granddaughter. They drank wine and bridged sixty years of life to reach an understanding.

For Peter

The Crocodile

The handsomest Crocodile in all the West
was a beautiful green with a pin-striped vest.
He wallowed in the pool then went on a quest
to attract the lady in the butter yellow dress.

He sped across the land as fast as he could;
she saw him coming and quite understood.
She ran for cover in the deep dark wood -
simply put, she was not in the mood.

He sidled up and blinked his eyes,
flicked his tail and told her lies.
He said his lake was gentian blue
with bloody meat enough for two.

He told her tales of snapping whole -
humans, horses and a sausage roll.
He said he'd give her lotus flowers,
build her waterfalls and towers.

She heaved a sigh, and took another peep;
he made more promises impossible to keep.
He bared his teeth, opened wide his jaw -
she smiled a little smile; she'd heard it all before.

She closed her eyes and pretended to sleep;
she wasn't going to fall besotted at his feet.
But he did look attractive in his pin-striped vest -
he was quite the yummiest crocodile in all the West!

Amelia

My name is Amelia, I'm not the flying type;
I haven't any wings and I hate the angel hype.
They were all the rage a while ago -
they turned up everywhere;
now they've disappeared
again into the strata-sphere.

Well angels never were my thing; I'm
firmly on the ground. My upside-down
bat cousins, all night they fly around.
And why they will hang upside down
I haven't got a clue,
but the nests they build with spittle
shine like morning dew.

My nests can also shine a-bright;
I collect all pretty things.
I like some sparkle sprinkled
amongst the twigs and things.
I'm a very busy fellow with a penchant for the new;
I build enormous middens from everything I chew.

Now this is quite acceptable to humans if I stay,
well within the forest, out of their precious way.
Apparently the humans do not like my chewing trait,
and if I move into their house, they yell, EXTERMINATE!

They lack a certain charity where pack rats are concerned;
they say I smell and make a noise; I really wish they'd learn
that they are not so perfect, they could attempt to share;
I've never thought of killing them - I haven't got the flare.

I thought I'd just get comfy, warm and better fed
if I moved in beside them - in a wall or garden shed.
I haven't any angels or any of their lore,
My wish is to survive them ... absolutely nothing more.

Mustela Nivilis Weasel

Mustela Nivilis, a Weasel for sure,
fast furious hunter - brave to the core.
Tenacious killer, passion aflame,
when the hunt is on enjoys the game.

Homo Sapiens, Human for sure,
a tally-ho hunter steeped in gore.
Across the world he's decimated
then come home and celebrated.

Hunting and killing is what they do,
Weasels, Humans but not the Gnu.
He doesn't go on a killing spree,
he's a Gourmet treat for a Lion's tea.

As long as someone in the deal
gets to eat another meal,
everything is hunky dory -
and that, said God, is end of story.

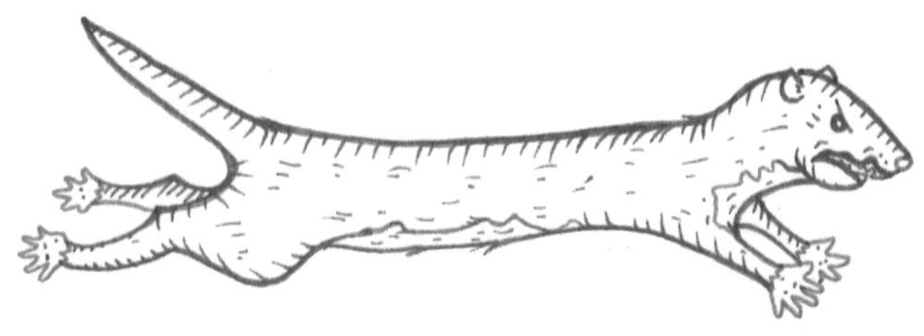

Annabelle Ant

Annabelle Ant was a very smart ant;
from the day she was born it was evident.

Amid thousands of
others she was a Queen -
for a million years,
an inherited gene.

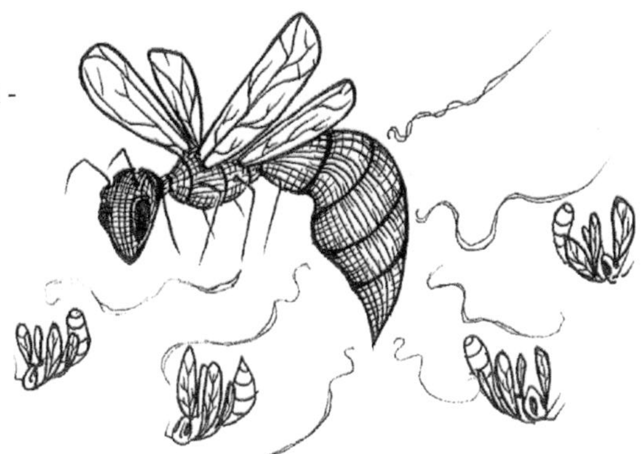

Her waist was slim,
her body large;
her antennae elegant
beyond just chance.

She knew she was beautiful, born to rule;
the wings she grew shone like dew.

Her perfume on her mating flight,
to every male was pure delight.

Aerobatics beyond desire,
raised to perfection the angels' choir.

The favoured male who'd done his best,
died on the wing with all the rest.

Annabelle landed and took a bow;
how to rule was obvious now.

She shed her wings with prim decorum,
determined to have a supportive quorum.

She'd learnt the rules of long-lived queens,
kill opposition by any means.

Basil

Basil bought a cat to kill the rat,
she would do what he wanted and that was that.
His friends kept telling him his chances were slim,
he would never own a cat, the cat would own him.

But Basil never listened, he knew it all,
as always happened he was heading for a fall.
The cat was a tabby with fierce green eyes
with an added expression he couldn't quite surmise.

She sat on a cushion, the best in the room,
he perched on a stool and began to assume.
Now this rat, Arabella, is why you are here,
you're a hunter not a pet,
am I making myself clear?

Arabella gazed at Basil,
and slowly blinked her eyes,
she gave a little yawn and started to rise.
She arched her back and turned around;
Basil re-assessed with the hint of a frown.

Arabella licked a paw and washed her face,
a casual titivation to put Basil in his place.
Arabella! shouted Basil, listen when I speak!
I want that rat gone by the end of the week!

Arabella jumped down from her cushion on the chair,
strolled slowly to the kitchen with a high and haughty air.
Basil followed after, anxious to point out,
Rat was in the cupboard - it was there without a doubt.

Arabella passed the cupboard on her way out to the door,
Basil really was impossible and such a crashing bore.
Basil followed after he didn't have a choice,
But he swore to himself in a very low voice.

He opened up the kitchen door and yelled, GET OUT!
Arabella waited- there was no need to shout.
She twitched her tail and smelled the air,
put out a cautious paw with tremendous care.

She was sensitive to weather and it felt like rain,
she hated to get wet, also dogs could be a pain.
So she hovered in the doorway till Basil lost his cool,
picked her up abruptly and dumped her on the stool.

Arabella Cat! he fumed, you sit right there!
Not on the cushion in my favourite chair!
She jumped right down - extremely hurt,
how insensitive he was - so vulgar and so curt.

She sulked on the cushion for at least a week,
he tempted her with fish, she refused to eat.
So he tried to appease her with saucers of milk,
Arabella - killing rats is not for cats of your ilk.

When he opened up a can of liver paté treat,
he realized with horror he was absolutely beat.
Arabella smiled, always gracious when she'd won,
and after all the hassle - well, it really had been fun.

So - let's forget the effing rat- it's really very plain,
the only thing they need is a bottle of champagne
to celebrate their future of mutual respect,
Arabella, boss of course, President Elect!

The Warthog

I'm a very handsome warthog and I'm almost bald;
my head is very large and very flat is what I'm told.
I have whiskers here and there, everywhere upon my skin -
which is very, very tough - a wrinkly sort of thing.
My mane is quite exceptional, lays well against my neck
nat-u-rally coiffed, it gives a cas-u-al effect.

A lighter sort of warthog, brown hair instead of black;
the bumps upon my head are astro-nom-ic-al-ly fat.
My eyes are set well high, some may say a little small,
but lashes long and luring, make up for any fall.
My tail is quite magnificent with its poncy puff of hair;
when perpendicular to the sky, it's simply debonair.

My upper tusks are ivory, curvaceously laid back;
my little ones are daggers - I kill if I'm attacked.
But on the whole I'm gentle, I'm quite benign in fact;
I kneel and graze on grasses, ox-peckers on my back.

A sturdy sort of animal, I live a family life;
I take an Aardvark's burrow and I'm meant to take a wife.
That sounds as though I'm lazy, but it's really not the case;
it's just that I'm nomadic - it's genetic to my race.

So I do not fight for territory - I would for mate and young;
but honestly I'm happier just grazing having fun.
But if I'm really threatened, caught and held at bay,
of course I'd fight to stay alive - but I'd rather run away.

So that is all I have to tell about a warthog doing well;
a warthog who is in his prime, a handsome fellow in the line.
One of a Sounder, tail held high, proud and beautiful to the sky.

POSTSCRIPT

I've heard it mentioned, but I'd rather forget,
that a Sounder of warthogs tails erect,
running through the bush in strict formation,
receives from humans a laughing ovation.
I have to say that in reply, a warthog often wonders why,
humans drive around the land, presuming to have all in hand.

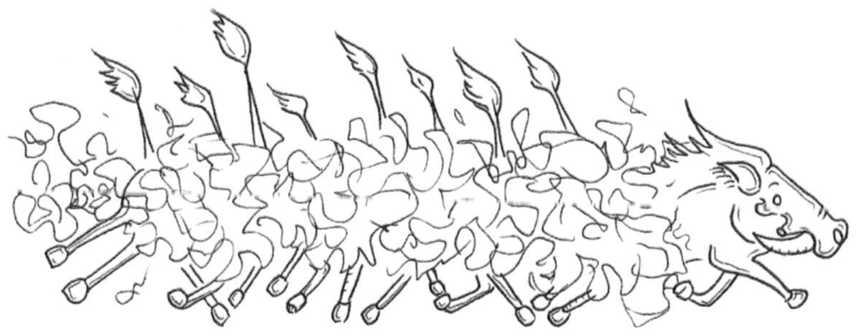

The Snail

A snail is a snail who lives in his shell,
if left alone does very well.
He dozes by day, he travels by night;
he leaves a trail of silvery light.

He goes very slowly and
people are rude;
they call him pokey
and some are crude.
He feels he goes at a rational pace;
he sees no need to join the race.

He doesn't care to twist and turn
to spin frenetically on a fern.
So he takes a bite of a luscious leaf
and continues on with a sigh of relief.

But when they say his silver shine
is nothing more than yucky slime,
he really is extremely hurt -
his whole existence turned to dirt.

He looks about for some relief;
he wobbles sadly on his leaf.
His horns aquiver feel the pain,
for snails, like us, are very vain.

But for now he will shrivel up,
pretend he hasn't felt the cut.
He'll stay inside his coiled shell
and think about it for a spell.

But a snub like that is quite
outrageous for shine medicinal
in the middle ages.
On second thoughts,
he *will* complain, to
George (Georgina)
down the lane.

Tilly Toad

Tilly Toad was fat and warty,
without a mate and nearly forty.
Goodness gracious, what a thing
to be so old without a ring
while other toads who weren't so pretty
swanned about the inner city,
laying double strands of eggs -
even those with bandy legs
had many beaus croaking lust -
Tilly really was nonplussed.

Then she had a bright idea,
everything became quite clear.
eHarmony was just the thing
for any girl to get a ring.
Her profile must be captivating,
likes and dislikes, right for dating.
She paid her dues and read the form
wrote a profile she thought was norm.

I'm young and fun and empathetic,
I love to jump; I'm quite athletic.
My toes are webbed, my eyes exotic,
and all my dreams are quite erotic.
A little bravado not amiss
for Tilly who had not been kissed.

Now in her needs for the right man
marriage and children was Tilly's plan.
An attractive lady not too stout
who wants a Toad to take her out.
A Toad of substance, not too small,
one with warts, brown skin and all.
One who jumps with sticky tongue,
a good provider for the young.
One with whom in spring she'll mate;
one with whom she'll hibernate.

Nervously she clicked on 'send'
and everyday went round the bend
looking at the men on line -
some of whom she thought were fine.
But when she met them in the bar,
they leered with lust and went too far.
Well, thought Tilly, perhaps I'm wrong
marriage and kids are for the strong.

And so her life she re-assessed,
she'd dress to kill and dance with zest.
She'd swan about the inner city
with all the men who found her pretty.
She didn't really want a ring;
she wanted life and lots of bling.
And after that, perhaps, who knows?
She'd settle down with one who chose
her empathy and not her clothes -
and they'd live together, just like Toads.

Stork

There was a stork named Sadie

When asked to fly said maybe.

She tried her best

To pass the test -

But always dropped the baby!

Parrot

Penelope parrot was crude and rude,
always in a rotten mood.
She had lived so long in paradise
before the hunter shot her twice.
So not surprising after a while,
traveling with him, mile after mile,
cramped and caged in a market square
she bit and scratched and didn't care.

Then a salty sailor picked her up,
paid too much but what the f#@k?
That was the word she learned to say,
the word she screeched, day after day.
The word that got her treats and claps
from all the crew, all the chaps.
Spoiled and encouraged while afloat,
Penelope loved her life on a boat!

Disembarkation at the dock
for a swearing Parrot was a shock.
The sailor took her to his Aunt;
a gift from the jungle he remarked.
Penelope screeched, F@#k! and Merde!
Aunt Emma fainted without a word.

The sailor sailed away next day;
Penelope was left to stay.
She looked around her new location,
regarded Emma with consternation.
Aunt Emma roused herself awake,
determined to deal with this mistake.

She stared the parrot in the eye,
you are not to swear, and I'll tell you why.
Your salty slang is just not cool;
we're going to have a language rule.
The parrot listened to her speech
then said the F word with a screech!

Oh no, said Emma, that will not do.
You were loud and saucy with the crew,
but here your life will be restrained;
you'll be a parrot completely tamed.
And that is what I think should be;
we will live together you and me.

And so they did for years and years;
embattled friends with love and tears.
When decades later, Emma died,
Penelope drooped, she sighed
she cried, until that sailor from the freighter,
the one who'd said,
see yer later!
came to pick Penelope up.
Penelope smiled and screeched out, 'F#@K!'

The Professor and the Mole

So you've been reading up on me
well, I've been studying you.
You think you know me inside out -
I'm not sure that is true.
So now I will expostulate -
introduce myself anew.

I'm really not an extrovert
except in early spring,
When I tunnel out to copulate -
it's a Darwin sort of thing.
With my captivating squeak I find a
mate for just a week,
Then tunnel home to be alone - without text or telephone.

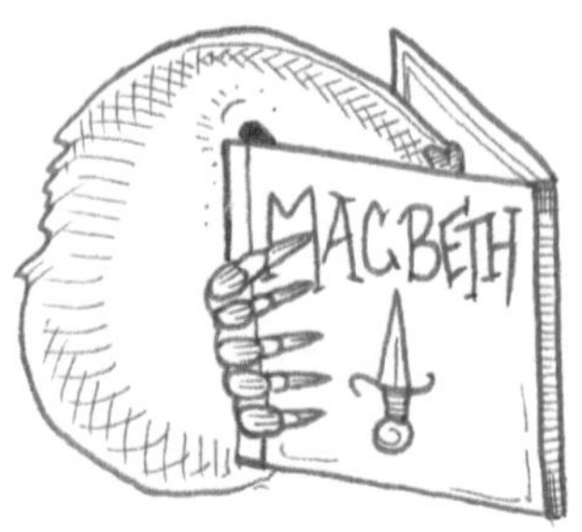

I love life underground;
it's a cozy sort of place,
several rooms for comfort,
and corridors for space.
Intruding moles not welcome -
I have fought one to the death;
exhausted then I rested,
with a copy of Macbeth.

You think my hearing compromised; well my ears are rather small.
There's a membrane covering my eyes, I can hardly see at all;
just light and dark, and sometimes, your shadow on the wall.
My pointed snout and little tail are brilliantly designed
to touch and smell acutely; I can usually survive.

As you see my legs are short but very, very strong;
my front ones are especially so my claws are super long.
I excavate my tunnels with unsurpassing speed;
20m a day is quite a range you must concede.

Dirt flies out behind me forming perfect little mounds,
in fields and fresh mown grasses where you say I'm out of bounds.
I like lawns that are manicured; what on earth is all the fuss?
I'm aerating, fertilizing - there's nothing to discuss!
I am needing soil that's suitable for digging rather deep
for living, nesting, wintering and going off to sleep.

I'm a fussy sort of fellow always tidying
up my home, while looking for the
juiciest, fattest, longest worm.
I keep a larder that is full of them
each head is bitten off-
They cannot stray, only stay–
Oh! Excuse me as I cough!

I feel I've lost your sympathy - well that's
a bit of gough, when you are setting traps
for me - let's call it quits, old Prof!

The Mosquito

Milly the Mosquito, when starving for a
meal
hunts for naked flesh, it is blood she wants
to steal.
But it's awfully hard to settle on a body
that is bare
when it's flailing out to swipe you, it's an open-ended dare.
But Millie's not a wimp, she is small and deadly keen -
she will scent you out and bite you if she thinks your
sweat her dream.
Nectar gives her energy and strengthens up her legs,
but a blood meal is essential for
the forming of her eggs.

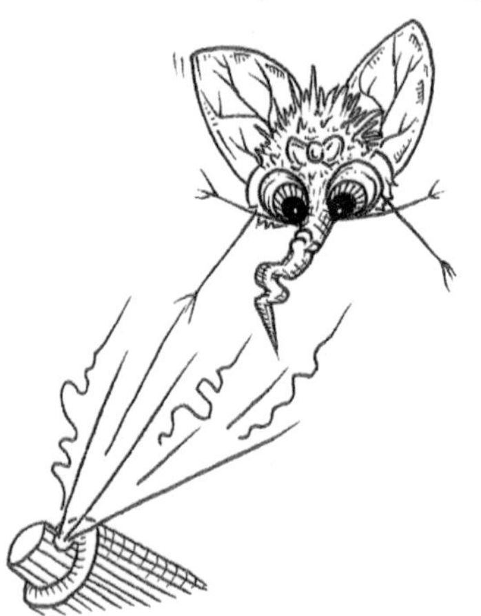

The Fish: A Life Story

I am a fish; I have a tail,
I swim in the depths; I tease a whale.
I dine on bits of this and that,
Blow champagne bubbles through my hat.

I am a fish with mermaid's tail;
I thought for a while I loved that whale.
But when he tried to dine on me,
I found him too salacious.

I am a fish with silver scales,
One hundred percent better than whales.
I spin with a shoal of metallic shine,
Cans of sardines, drunk on wine.

I look through my mirror and see the sun,
Rip tides dancing; I join the fun.
I travel knots till the light goes in,
Silhouettes only, the light is dim.

Below the waves in
a stormy sea,
I'm safe with an
octopus having tea;
He changes colour,
looking at me.

I am a fish with enormous eyes,
A bit short sighted, but never mind.
I see the colours of coral reefs,
Colours quite beyond belief.

Hermit crabs and tidal drifts,
Seaweed gardens,
Neptune's gifts.

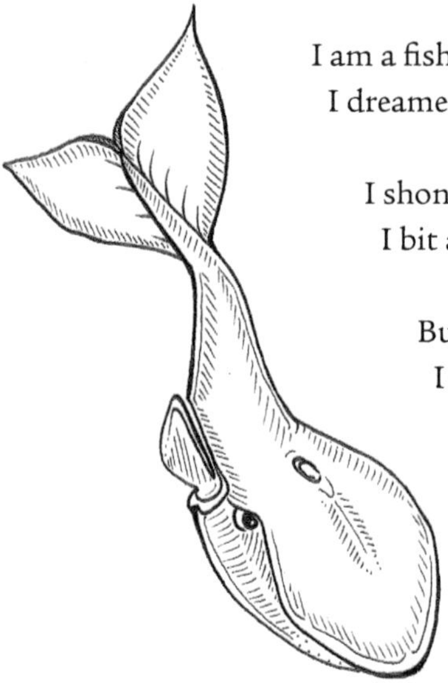

I am a fish with silvery sheen
I dreamed of all I could have been.

I shone in the moonlight luminesque,
I bit at sunbeams; I did my best.

But like that mermaid on a rock,
I really should have taken stock;

I never dreamed, I never wished
to be a fillet on a dish!

MILK
SUGAR

Cat and Mouse

Cat licked her paws and washed her face;
of another little mouse, she had left no trace.
She preened outside her larder door,
live and fresh, plenty more.

A mouse poked his head out from the hole in the wall;
Cat put his paw out as if to maul.
Mouse twitched his nose in fearful disdain,
gave a little squeak and went inside again.

Cat blinked her eyes and pretended to preen;
Mouse started shaking, he turned a little green.
It's very upsetting, a Cat outside your house;
to calm his nerves, he would play a little Strauss.

Music always helped him in times of stress;
The Moonlight Sonata was usually the best.
But on this occasion, he needed more bravado,
more tightening up of sinew -
more definite machado.

Vigorously fraught,
he screeched his bow across the strings;
his little body quivered,
his whiskers twirled in rings.
The more he played Strauss,
the more excited he became,
Spinning, Swizzling,
Pirouetting - dizzily insane.

Cat meanwhile was dozing in a sunbeam on the floor;
she'd had enough to eat - she wasn't hungry anymore.
She was far too warm with belly full to bother with a mouse;
she was satisfied she'd taught him who was lady of the house.

Mistake

What a silly mistake for a god to make
to give the world to man.
You would have thought
He'd have taken more care,
After the snake and the apple affair!

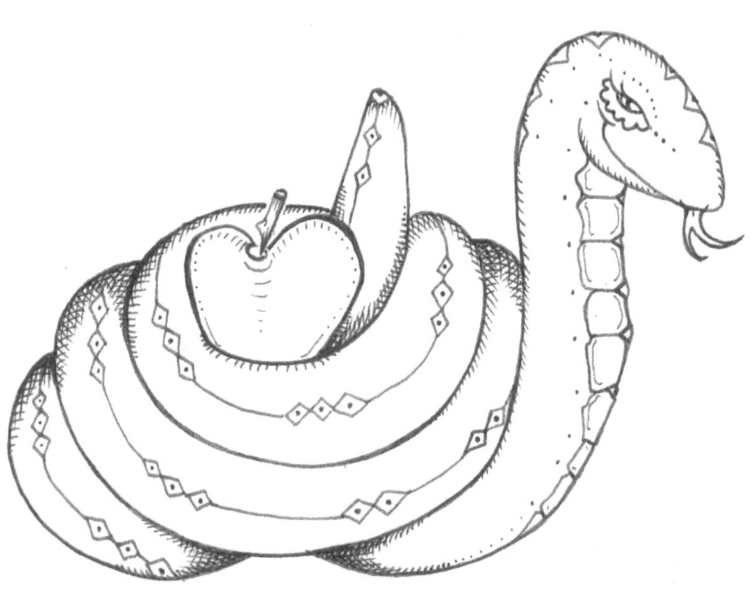

Acknowledgements

To my daughter, Louise, for her Herculean effort to be patient with her mother and without whose encouragement, perseverance and hard work there would be no book.

To my son, Richard, who helped when no one was looking.

To family and friends, a big thank you for patiently listening to yet another rhyme.

www.ingramcontent.com/pod-product-compliance
Ingram Content Group UK Ltd.
Pitfield, Milton Keynes, MK11 3LW, UK
UKHW042002190726
13854UKWH00005B/2116